A GIRL WITH A BOOK

by Nick Wood

Published by Playdead Press 2013

© Nick Wood 2013

Nick Wood has asserted his rights under the Copyright, Design and Patents Act, 1988, to be identified as the author of this work.

A CIP catalogue record for this book is available from the British Library.

ISBN 978-1-910067-00-0

Caution
All rights whatsoever in this play are strictly reserved and application for performance should be sought through the author before rehearsals begin. No performance may be given unless a license has been obtained.

This book is sold subject to the condition that it shall not by way of trade or otherwise, be lent, resold, hired out, or otherwise circulated without the publisher's prior consent in any form of binding or cover other than that in which it is published and without a similar condition including this condition being imposed on the subsequent purchaser.

Printed by BPUK

Playdead Press
www.playdeadpress.com

A GIRL WITH A BOOK

A Girl with a Book was first performed at The Neville Studio, Nottingham Playhouse on June 10th 2013.

The Writer   Nick Wood

Director   Andrew Breakwell.

The play is set in the room where the writer works. The writer can be played by an actor of any age, ethnicity or gender.

Nick Wood

Plays include *Warrior Square, Mia, Birdboy, My Name is Stephen Luckwell, A Dream of White Horses.* – Nick began his career as an actor, became a teacher before leaving teaching to write full time. His commissions include the Crucible, Theatr Iolo, Radio 4, Eastern Angles, and Nottingham Playhouse. His work has been performed extensively in Europe where he has been commissioned by the Thalia Theater, Hamburg, the Hans Otto Theater, Potsdam and Kazaliste Voriovitica in Croatia. He is an RSC Learning Associate.

Andrew Breakwell

Andrew was the Director of Roundabout and Education at Nottingham Playhouse from 1999 to 2012, prior to that he was Associate Director at the New Wolsey Theatre, Ipswich and has he also worked at York Theatre Royal, the Wilde Theatre in Bracknell and at the Stephen Joseph Theatre in Scarborough. Andrew has directed over 200 productions including - *The Caretaker, The Silver Sword, Tom's Midnight Garden* and *Roots*.

It's Sunday, October 13th 2013. In the Observer main section there's an article on the dangers of commodifying Malala, in the arts pages there's a review of her book, I Am Malala. This week, a year to the day she was shot, she's been awarded the EU Sakharov Prize, been nominated for the Noble Peace Prize, which she didn't get, much to the delight of the T.T.P. the Pakistan Taliban –

"We are delighted that she didn't get it," said group spokesman Shahidullah Shahid. "She did nothing big so it's good that she didn't get it. This award should be given to the real Muslims who are struggling for Islam. Malala is against Islam, she is secular."

You can't help feeling they've missed the point.

She's been all over the radio and TV and in the States on the Today Show her lack of bitterness towards those who tried to kill her rendered the host Jon Stewart speechless.

A year ago I started to write a play about the attempt to kill her and this weekend, fresh out of rehearsals, I'm trying to write a preface for the programme text for A Girl With A Book, and I'm not sure where to begin.

The more I thought about what I wanted to say, the more it became clear that it wasn't going to be only about Malala and the shooting. It was a terrible act. The first thought I had when I read about it on the afternoon of 9th October last year was this is ludicrous. I couldn't comprehend how anyone could contemplate doing such a thing, let alone carry it out. In May I had the same feelings with regard to the senseless slaughter of Lee Rigby in Greenwich. If I wanted to do anything it was to find a way to articulate those feelings and the confusion they engendered.

I'm not a pacifist, my father and his generation served in WW2 and had I been alive, and I'm profoundly grateful that I wasn't, I know I'd have had to do the same. Since my last playground scrap I've never committed an act of violence, but if me and my family were attacked I can imagine that I'd try to fight back. I've seen violence and I know that war, no matter how justifiable the cause isn't noble, it's sordid, cruel and degrading. So there are things that if forced to I would fight for, but there's a whole list of those for which I wouldn't and top of that list is religion. I believe that those who are the victims of religious intolerance should be defended but I can't see why anyone would want to attack and kill another person because they believe in a different story.

Before the shooting I knew pretty much nothing about Malala, if asked about the Taliban or Muslim extremists I'd have said I had no sympathy for a religious group that felt the need to impose their medieval views on the rest of us. I was appalled by their treatment of women but it all felt so distant and insoluble that I suppose I wished as I did at the height of the Troubles in Northern Ireland that it would all go away.

I had the concept from the start. It was the first thing I wrote after the title.

   The writer — can be played by an actor of any age, gender, or ethnicity.

But to start with the writer was going to be played by me. What did I think I was trying to do? My doubts nearly scuppered the project before it began.

- It's a vanity project.
- I'll be seen as trying to ride on the back of a terrible event.
- I have nothing to add to the debate.
- I have no right to think I can contribute.
- I am completely the wrong person to do this.
- It's an act of appalling hubris.
- I can't do it.

Gradually as the notes and scribbles turned into drafts, and I moved away from books and the internet and started to talk to people of faith and make tentative approaches towards the Muslim community I realised that it wasn't only about Malala. It touched on how art can comment on real events, how the writer has to find objectivity when little exists in the writer's mind, the way that Muslims have been swiftly and subtly objectified as the next group to be blamed for everything, how I was seeing people as members of a group and not as individuals, and no matter how much I might protest to the contrary and hold up my liberal principles as proof of my lack of prejudice the *differentness* of a set of beliefs I didn't share was becoming an almost insuperable barrier to my willingness to try and understand a world removed from my own, but one I couldn't ignore.

Putting all the research and prejudice and lack of understanding into the play was hard. To start with it came out as a series of disjointed rants. The director, Andrew Breakwell, helped me cut and focus the text. I started to leave more and more out, suggesting a point rather than hammering it home.

I wanted to keep the exact words said by Malala and her father and anyone I spoke to only allowing myself to select and edit, but I also wanted the writer to lose the sense of being me. In the course of writing a scene involving real people without thinking I made up an incident that was supposed to have happened to the writer as a child. It was a break through moment and from then on in the writing and in rehearsal I think the writer slowly became a character.

I wrote *A Girl With A Book* because I had to. Because I'd been a teacher, because I'd never heard a child speak so passionately about the need for education, because amongst the whole global catalogue of appalling acts I'd never heard of anyone shooting three children for wanting to go to school. When I nearly packed it in I carried on because I wanted to work through all the attitudes and prejudices it stirred up within me that I was so anxious to deny.

Nick Wood

Acknowledgements

I'd like to thank Giles Croft and Nottingham Playhouse whose support has been invaluable. Andrew Breakwell who kept me focussed. All those people of faith and no faith who have talked to me, listened to me, and pointed me in the right direction when I lost my way. And always, Anne and Alice, who despite me giving them plenty of reasons to do otherwise, have always believed.

Nick Wood

A GIRL WITH A BOOK.

A chair with a desk and a laptop on it. Another chair downstage. A small rug in front of the desk. Books, pamphlets, notebooks, folders, newspaper cuttings are on the desk, on the floor. Behind the desk is a third chair with a cardboard box on it. The writer comes in with a cup of coffee. Sits. Checks his notebook. Checks through the print out of Malala's blog. Stretches and begins to tap the keys. He's concentrating but it doesn't seem as though he's writing.

Bugger!

I don't care what anyone says – I am working. This is work. You ask any writer. You can't expect the words to come pouring out all day long. It doesn't happen like that – you can get stuck. Then if you do something else, something mindless, like playing a spider solitaire, if you're lucky, suddenly out of nowhere an idea can pop into your head and the problem's solved itself. Not everyone understands that. My wife'll come up here – and say -

Couldn't the something mindless be something that's useful at the same time?

Like what?

Putting the hoover round the house? Mowing the lawn? Sorting out the tap in the bathroom you were going to fix months ago?

You're missing the point. You have to concentrate to... hoover. What spider solitaire allows me to do is let my mind go completely blank...

It's a bit like meditation really. No, it's not. It's time wasting.

I can tell you when exactly. Half past four. 9th October. Last year. I'd been writing all day. Pages and pages. None of them any good. Decided that was it and deleted the lot.

He clicks onto the BBC website and reads.

Malala Yousafzai: Pakistan activist, 14, shot in Swat

Gunmen have wounded Malala Yousafzai, a 14-year-old rights activist who has campaigned for girls' education in the Swat Valley in north-west Pakistan.

A fourteen year old girl shot for wanting to go to school?

Two other girls were shot. Kainat Riaz and Shazia Ramzan, got hit as well. Malala in the head. Kainat in the shoulder. Shazia below her left collarbone and in her left hand as she tried to protect herself. Four bullets. Fired point blank into the back of a school bus by a man in a balaclava. Why would anyone do a thing like that? There's a statement out already. From the TTP, who are...? The Pakistani Taliban.

The TTP successfully targeted Malala Yousafzai. Although she was young and a girl and the TTP does not believe in attacking women, whoever leads a campaign against Islam & Shariah is ordered to be killed by Shariah. If anyone thinks that Malala is targeted because of education, that's absolutely wrong, and propaganda from the media.

Madness.

For crying out loud, she's only fourteen. And they think they can justify what they've done in the name of religion? Well, they're not the first ones to try that one. Make your own list. Fourteen.

Who is she? How did this happen?

He gets up from the desk.

> I knew that night I wanted to write... something. When you first get an idea your mind starts racing with all the possibilities. It should be simple. I've got the story. The trick'll be to find the right way in. And then, a few days later Ban Ki Moon came out with this - *The terrorists showed what frightens them most: a girl with a book.* He's given me the title. All I've got to do is... write it.

I made notes, I made coffee. I went on Google, I walked the dog. I read books about Pakistan and Islam. I might even have played the odd game of spider solitaire. But A Girl With A Book. Cast of four, 3 female/1 male. Male actor to double Malala's father and the gunman – it's not going to work, doesn't feel right.

I played around with it off and on for a week before I ground to a halt with a blank page and a question. What have I, a white, middle aged, middle class playwright of no fixed belief, living safely in the west, got to say on a subject about which I know nothing at all?

You can't do everything via Google. No, you can't. Really. I'm going to have to go out. Talk to people. Ask questions. Approach the whole thing with an open mind. Except... I have this sneaking suspicion the last thing I've got is an open mind.

I start with the Islamic information stall outside Marks & Spencers – May I ask a question?

Do you know, sir, the first question we always get asked about Islam? Why do we men make Muslim women dress like they do?

I wasn't going to ask that actually, but now you mention it, I don't really get it either.

When you see a woman, sir, in the street, and she is all exposed, you look at her. You can't help yourself. I'm a married man, but I look too. If that woman is covered, then we don't see her only as an object of sexual desire.

I don't think women should be treated only as objects of sexual desire, but if they are, it's not the woman's fault, is it, it's the man's? Look, I was in Washington in the summer, it was blazing hot...

I know what you are going to say, sir.

There's this Muslim family, the husband, children, all wearing light summer clothes. Except the wife. She's in black from head to foot, even her eyes are behind a gauze screen. She must have been dying in there.

But that woman understands her discomfort is nothing compared to the heat she would have to endure if she went straight into the fires of hell.

What can you say? I don't argue. I can't. We chat some more. At least we can agree the way Muslims are suddenly to blame for everything is wrong and bad for us all. I want to try to understand but we're miles apart. We smile, shake hands, and I thank him as I walk away with a copy of the Koran and an armful of books on Islam.

The fires of hell for dressing in appropriate summer clothing?

And he got me too. 'Do you know the first question we always get asked about Islam?' That wasn't going to be my first question.

I mean everyone's free to dress how they like but there's no sense to it. Even if you say it's your choice you're covering up why wouldn't you want to feel the rain on your face and the wind in your hair? And it *is* always men telling women what to do.

But what does make sense? Tattoos? Top hats? Getting your nose pierced? Bishops and cardinals in frocks? I've got no objection to nuns and they cover their heads.

There's lots of stuff I don't get about organised religion. For one, they're all so keen on sin and punishment. They talk about compassion. Mercy. Forgiveness. But you don't seem to see very much of it, do you? Catholics and Protestants have been killing each other for centuries. They're all at it. In Burma we've got Buddhists killing Muslims – Buddhists for God's sake? And…

This is not getting anything written.

He goes back to the desk.

But what if you do feel you are the ones always getting blamed for everything? What if you and your family live with the daily threat of being killed by bombs dropped from unmanned drones?

Can't be much fun over here. You wear the hijab. You've got a beard. I bet you can feel people looking at you everywhere you go.

He gets up. He can't settle to work.

It's so tangled. I can't make sense of what I feel about any of it. Don't get me wrong, I'm not prejudiced. I can't be, can I? I read the Guardian.

You know those sentences that start I'm not racist / sexist / homophobic / whatever else the speaker wants you to believe they aren't and then they stick in the word *but* and go on to prove that's exactly what they are?

Yeah, well, my sentence would have to be - I'm all for diversity but wouldn't the world be a much simpler and safer place if everybody thought like me?

Then I get it. Of course I've got to do the research, but I don't have to beat myself up because I don't know everything there is to know about Islam and Pakistan. I can still tell the story. What it's about is what it's always been about - ordinary people doing extraordinary things. I'll still go out and talk to those who know more about it than I do. Maybe I can get some of them to let me try bits out on them. But I'll put away the books until I need them. Get rid of google, and go back to the beginning. 2009. The eleven year old Malala, at home with her family in Mingora, a small town in the Swat Valley.

It's night time. Evening prayers are over. Malala's playing games on the computer with her brother. She looks at her Harry Potter rucksack and her blue uniform hanging from a hook on the back of the door. She thinks about what she's going to wear to school.

I can't wear my school uniform, I can't wear my pink dress because the Taliban will think it's too colourful.

Her father Ziauddin listens. He's the principal of the girls' school so he's her head teacher as well her dad. He takes a piece of paper out of his pocket. It's a print out of a blog from the BBC Urdu website written by a girl called Gul Makai. He reads it to them -

'My mother made me breakfast and I went off to school. I was afraid going to school because the Taleban had issued an edict banning all girls from attending schools. Only 11 students attended the class out of 27. Perhaps there will be more tomorrow.'

'A friend of mine gave me this today. He told me to read it. I wanted to say Gul Makai is really my daughter. Your mother thinks we should change your name to Gul Makai. She thinks it's a much nicer name than Malala.'

Malala was a warrior, I'd rather be named after a hero, than a cornflower, says her brother.

That's because you're a boy and all you can think about is fighting, says his sister.

Shall I read some more? Asks her father.

Time for bed, says her mother.

She bustles the children away, leaving the last paragraph of the blog unread...

He returns to the desk and finds the print out of the blog and reads it out.

> 'On my way from school to home I heard a man saying 'I will kill you'. I hastened my pace and after a while I looked back if the man was still coming behind me. But to my utter relief he was talking on his mobile and must have been threatening someone else over the phone.'

Eleven years old when she wrote that. Another girl was supposed to do it but she changed her mind, and Ziauddin put forward his daughter to take her place.

Could I have asked my daughter to write that blog?

He finds another passage in the printed blog.

I have a heavy bag, I go to school, I come home, I do my homework...

He steps away from the desk remembering Ziauddin's words.

My daughter complained about school, but when it was banned she knew how much she wanted it.

People said to me: How can you let her do this? We had to stand up. She knew what would come. We saw many atrocities, many cruelties. When the elders are silent, the children have to speak up.

When the elders are silent, the children have to speak up...

I take the couple of pages I've written so far into a year ten English class at a girls' school to see what they think. And to ask that question: If I were Ziauddin, what would I have done?

A face in the front row looks up at me from under her hijab and listens as the other girls put forward their opinions.

- You'd have to live there to know...

- It's a different way of life…

- Different culture …

- Perhaps she wanted to do it…

Then she puts up her hand to speak. Brought up in Libya. She knows more than I'll ever know about living with danger. '*When you know that everywhere you go, I'm not sure how to say this, death is walking very near to you, you are afraid, but you think differently about life, about being alive. It's important, but not so important.*'

A few weeks later I'm trying out a new section with a group of community workers when, after the first few pages, a striking black woman takes out a notepad and starts writing. Right in front of me. I try to ignore her and concentrate on the others but my eyes keep being drawn back. What's she writing? A shopping list? I'm willing her - put down the pen and listen to me. When I've finished she's the first one to speak. '*What that girl said, about death walking near you, I know that pain. It made me remember. I wrote something. Sorry. But I had to.*' She and her family were badly beaten up by the National Front in the eighties. She reads me what she was writing –

'*You have to stand up. Why hide? Hiding is more painful. Like being in darkness. When you stop hiding it's freedom. You stand up and walk in the light. What price is freedom? How much is the cost for freedom? Maybe a life?'*

When will I stop jumping to conclusions about people? The last time I stood up for anything I was ten years old and Martin Mayfield had tried to pinch my bike.

Where does anyone find that kind of courage?

I go back on line and start watching the interviews. In one she's sitting next to her father, talking about what she wants to be when she grows up when he interrupts her.

I want to be a doctor that is my dream.

I think she could do so much more. She should become a politician. People would listen to her. She should work to build a society where any girl can become a medical student and finish her studies.

Her face says, that's his dream, not mine. Ziauddin talks about why he won't leave Swat, the debt he owes to the valley and its people, and how if he has to die honouring that debt then he can't think of a better way. He asks her - What do you think about those nights when I don't sleep here? In the house? In case they come looking for me?

She makes this little noise and hides her head in her hands. She's frightened. Then she looks up, straight at the camera. Nobody's going to make that girl do something she doesn't want to, not even her dad.

What's it like in Swat? I've got no mental picture.

He types.

Images of the Swat valley. It's beautiful. I didn't expect this - all these adverts. Luxury hotels, holiday homes, adventure holidays, skiing, white water rafting. It's got the lot. Until 2009, when the Taliban arrive.

There are still rows of tables with starched white napkins in the Continental Hotel but no guests. There are colourful piles of silk in the China Market, but no customers. A banner hangs over the entrance – 'Women are requested to avoid shopping in China Market.'

Public floggings are announced. Attendance expected. There are executions at the crossroads. One night, on the radio, they hear this.

He plays the Taliban warning of the closure of girls' schools on his I phone.

After January 15th girls must not go to school otherwise the guardians and the schools will be held responsible.

50,000 girls will be staying at home. To go, almost overnight from being the ideal tourist destination to that...

Why so frightened about educating women? Nobody's throwing acid at women who want to go to university but I don't think we've got a particularly brilliant record over here.

He goes on line. Types.

Women's education. 1897 riots in Cambridge. When it looked like women might be allowed to become full members of the university men marched through the streets pelting women suspected of being students with rotten fruit, some were stoned.

1921 – more riots – when women are awarded degrees the same the men.

Types.

Women's rights. UK. Timeline.

It took the suffragettes till 1918 to get the vote. Then another ten years before women could vote at the same age as men. Up to 1944 a woman had to leave teaching if she got married. Until 1975 you could sack a woman for being pregnant. And so it goes on. Yeah, and that's right, I was talking to somebody the other week who said Boots got it in the neck for putting toys from the Science

Museum in the boys section but not in the girls. And this is 2013.

Why did the Taliban move into Swat?

Goes to his notes.

Close to the safety of the mountains and the border. Good base for attacks on Islamabad. Classic guerilla tactics. But the rich and powerful had their holiday villas in Swat so it was never going to be long before the army was called in.

The schools are closed. The fighting's getting closer. What was she thinking?

He finds the blog and reads it.

I wake up to the roar of heavy artillery fire early in the morning. I'm bored with sitting at home. Some of my friends have already left Swat. It's very dangerous. I can't leave home. I can't go out. I wish my father would take us away from here.

He starts to imagine the scene. He sits and begins to type as he speaks.

Tomorrow we're leaving.

Where are we going?

To Islamabad.

He stops typing but stays at the desk, imagining the voices in the scene.

> *The one good thing about the war is that our father has taken us to many other cities. Islamabad, Peshawar, Bannu. And now we are staying with my aunt. It's good to sit in her garden, watching my brothers play, feeling the silence and the peace. My father comes into the garden. He wants my little brother.*

Malala, where's your brother?

Playing.

What's he doing?

I don't know.

He's digging a hole. Why is he digging a hole?

Ask him.

Hey? What are you doing? What's the game? Why are you digging a hole in uncle's lawn?

I'm making a grave.

What's that little boy seen to make him want to play at grave digging?

Three weeks later they're back home in Mingora. Someone's broken into their house but the only thing missing is the TV. Her uniform and school bag are hanging where she left them and to her brothers disgust their school opens tomorrow. A truce is called. The fighting stops. Peace talks start. People come back onto the streets. Shops open. Women return to the China Market. But if the extremists have disappeared they haven't gone far. A journalist who took a stand against them is killed, their threats are still on the radio. And the identity of the school girl who wrote a blog for the BBC is no longer a secret.

How could it be kept a secret? She put in too much personal detail. Where she went with her parents. Her friends at school getting bored with hearing about her trip to Bunbair. Didn't anyone at the BBC say, hang on, if you put that bit in everyone will know it's you? Perhaps they did. Perhaps she didn't want them to change a word.

He goes to his notebook and reads.

Nowhere does it say that girls should not be allowed to go to school. I have my right to play, to sing, to talk, to go to the market, to stand up. I will have my dream. I will have my education.'

She's on TV, she's on chat shows, she's interviewed on news programmes, she's awarded the Pakistan Youth Prize. She's famous. Come on, it must have been exciting.

Watch the videos and you're watching a child grow up. Far too soon. Far too fast.

He checks in his notebook.

The Taliban are back. And this time the army are in earnest. Warnings go out, giving the day and the time the bombardment will start. The rich leave first, followed by thousands of refugees desperate to get away from the fighting. The Yousafzai family go with them. They'll be away for three months.

The children and their mother go to relatives. Ziauddin goes to Pashawar with other senior figures from Swat to lobby the government. He shares a room with two other men. One room where they eat, sleep, pray, and plan their strategy. Every day they are out meeting politicians, addressing crowds in the street, organising press conferences, orchestrating the protests.

'A mother doesn't give milk to a baby that doesn't cry – you have to scream for everything!'

The Taliban announce Ziauddin is now a target. It doesn't stop him, he and his friends keep up the pressure, but they're feeling the strain of being away from their wives and children.

- We get bored with each other.

- The three of us in the same room.

- Always talking about the same things.

Then Ziauddin does something no father should ever do.

He has forgotten my birthday. I told him yesterday it was my birthday tomorrow. I have a birthday cake for me. My birthday has been celebrated. He's not here. I am happy for the people who made me the cake, but I am not happy for him.

She has sent me a text in English. She is not happy with me. She wants ice cream, I shall see her soon and I shall take her for ice cream. There's so much to do. The campaign to free Swat. I am optimistic. I am very optimistic. I believe that things will change. I believe that the Taliban will go from Swat. They will be defeated.

Malala has a new ambition. '*I have changed my dream from being a doctor to being a politician because I want to help my people*' She shares her father's dreams but she sees him more clearly now. Even though the army says they've defeated the Taliban she has her doubts. '*He is too optimistic. I have a fear in my heart that the Taliban can re – collect their power.*'

Father and daughter meet again on the road home. And I find this amazing. Considering the danger they're in. They stop. Ziauddin and the other leaders have a meeting with Richard Holbrook. The American ambassador. He brings Malala with him. She takes part. She asks for help '*I request you all, and I request you, Mr Ambassador, if you will help us with our education.*' It's not a secret meeting either. It's filmed by the cameras that have been following them around for months. That's how we know that afterwards Malala goes shopping for DVDs and, at last, she gets her ice cream.

Mingora's deserted, the school's been used as a military base, there are shell holes in the walls, but their house is still standing and her school books are still there. Almost as soon as they get back, the film is put on the internet. By The New York Times. How did they think that was going to go down? Cooperating with America. If you're living next to a wasps' nest what's the first thing you do? Go up and poke it with a stick?

She's only twelve years old and she's become a political activist. Oh, and then did the hate came pouring out.

'She is a symbol of the infidels and obscenity.'

You see this girl. Writing for the BBC. Being filmed by an American journalist for an American newspaper. Being praised by the American president.

He gets up.

> If I was living on the border of Pakistan? Would my anger against those who're dropping the bombs turn itself on Malala because I saw her as being on their side? Possibly. Would I think she was being used? Probably. Would I consider killing her to be a righteous act? No. And when the TTP tried neither did the millions who poured onto the streets in protest.
>
> If unmanned drones were flying over my home Thackeray's Lane, and my family was in danger of being killed by a misdirected bomb you'd find it hard to win over my heart and mind.

He looks for a printout of Malala's statements and reads them, remembering the things Ziauddin said as he does so.

> *I think of what might happen often and imagine the scene clearly. Even if they come to kill me, I will tell them what they are trying to do is wrong, that education is our basic right.*
>
> Nothing's going to shut them up. Her or her dad.
>
> Girls' education is not considered as important as boys' education.
>
> *Girls will be able to go to school. I will have my education.*

The reality is that girl's education is not only under threat from terrorism.

I think if the President's daughters went to school in Swat the schools would not have been closed.

You must give a daughter all her basic rights.

I will have my dream.

The bell rings for the end of the school day. It's a Tuesday. Tuesday's are safe. You feel nervous on a Friday, not a Tuesday, because Friday is the day of prayer and some believe if you sacrifice yourself on a Friday when you arrive in paradise you will be all the more blessed.

Fourteen girls and three teachers climb into the school bus, an open truck, a canvas cover over the bench seats keeps off the sun and a blue curtain flapping at the back keeps out some of the dust.

They have prepared for this day. The route has been studied. They know when the bus will leave. Where it will stop. How long it will take on each stage of its journey. They have chosen their spot carefully. A car waits to take them into the mountains and across the border.

The bus comes slowly round a sharp bend. The next stop will be Malala's. Less than two hundred metres past the military checkpoint, within plain sight of the soldiers, the bus comes to a halt. The girls can't see the gunmen who've fired the warning shots that made the driver stop and they mistake those shots for the sound of the engine misfiring.

The curtain is pulled back and a man in a black balaclava asks

Where is Malala? Who is Malala?

We thought it was a joke, a story from a dream.

They will have recognised her, anyone can recognise her, we used to cover our faces but she never covered hers.

The moment she said 'I am Malala' he opened fire, and she was down.

Four bullets. Three girls. Kainat, Malala, Shazia. He missed his target three times. He was only a few feet away from her. What was he thinking as he pointed his gun at a bus load of children? Did his hand shake?

The gunmen escape and the girls are rushed to the nearest hospital. Malala, the most seriously hurt, goes straight into intensive care. They stabilise her and as soon as it's safe to, she's airlifted, Ziauddin at her side, to a military hospital in Peshawar for emergency surgery.

He sits in the chair S/L. Looks up as if he was looking at the gunman. Flinches and ducks down.

> She must have been leaning forward. Ducking for cover.

He goes to the chair behind the desk and takes a polystyrene head wrapped in a scarf out of the cardboard box, puts it on the desk and unwraps it. He pushes a pencil into the hole he's made to illustrate the path of the bullet, turns, and holds it up.

> The bullet came downwards, missing her brain, shattering her ear, grazing her jaw, and taking away a piece of her skull. The surgeons clean up the wound and tuck the piece of bone inside her abdomen, keeping it safe, alive, in case it was decided to graft it back onto her head. Isn't that clever?

> She can move her arms and legs but no-one can say if she'll live. They've done what they can, but she needs specialist facilities, expert treatment. Sedated and on a ventilator she's flown to Rawalpindi…

He wraps the head in the scarf and puts it back in the box.

> …and then, finally, to the Queen Elizabeth Hospital in Birmingham where they've become world experts on treating the kind of wounds

Malala has suffered. They've had to - it's where they send the most seriously injured British service men and women.

Her family are with her in the hospital. The news of her progress is good. She can talk, she is able to hear with her one good ear. She can take a few steps. Her brain is still exposed, so the biggest danger will be from infection. They send her home, to rest, to get strong enough for the next step.

Some weeks later she's back in hospital ready for the operation that will rebuild her shattered ear and repair the hole in her skull. The bone they planted in her abdomen has shrunk, and may shrink further. To graft it on now would mean more operations in the future.

He picks up a saucer, tips the paper clips onto the desk and uses it to illustrate what they intend to do with the plate.

Instead the technicians make a titanium plate for the surgeons to fit over the hole in her skull. Both operations are successful. After months of living with a hole in her head, her exposed brain has been covered. She will be well again.

He puts the paper clips back in the saucer and goes behind the desk.

Malala and her family aren't the only heroes. While she was in hospital in Birmingham the thirteen other girls who were on the bus went back to school.

He picks up and reads the statements from the three girls.

'I love to study, and nothing will stop me,' said Kainat, 'not even a bullet.'

'Even if they attack me three more times,' said Shazia, I will always go back to school.'

The suspected gunman, a chemistry graduate from Swat, escaped over the border to Afghanistan. His sister, Rehanna Haleem, who still lives in Swat spoke about her brother.

He has brought shame on our family, what he did was intolerable. I don't consider him my brother anymore.

That's courage.

He gets up from behind the desk.

I'm getting closer to writing this thing I know it. I could start writing it now but for all this other stuff going round in my head. The questions. The TTP have one - I know, they're the ones who tried to kill her, but it doesn't stop it being a good question. If we care so much about Malala and her friends why don't we make as much noise about all those the children who are dying whose names we don't know? Especially as some of them are probably being killed by drones controlled by someone in an office on an airfield in Lincolnshire.

This event is different. And to acknowledge that difference doesn't diminish the suffering that others experience. Kainat, Shazia, and Malala weren't innocent victims caught in a bombing raid, or wounded by shell fire not meant for them. They were targeted because a child stood up and said – this is wrong and she made people listen. You can call it defending your religion, you can call it a war, you can call it a jihad, you can call it what you like. But you don't shoot three girls for wanting to go to school.

The writer sees the note he's made about Ziauddin. He reads it.

'I'm optimistic about the behaviour of men towards their daughters. We have so many fathers, so many brothers who want education for their sisters and their daughters.'

He picks up the statement from Malala and reads it.

Why shouldn't girls go to school? I want my education. I want to go to university. Education is a right for me. It is a right for all the girls in Swat, in Pakistan, in the world.

Fingers crossed.

He stretches and starts to write. Stops and stares straight ahead.

End